Chief of Sinners

Chief of Sinners

Michelle Andre'

authorHOUSE®

AuthorHouse™
1663 Liberty Drive
Bloomington, IN 47403
www.authorhouse.com
Phone: 1-800-839-8640

Published by AuthorHouse 12/16/2014

ISBN: 978-1-4969-5497-8 (sc)
ISBN: 978-1-4969-5483-1 (e)

Library of Congress Control Number: 2014920881

Any people depicted in stock imagery provided by Thinkstock are models, and such images are being used for illustrative purposes only. Certain stock imagery © Thinkstock.

This book is printed on acid-free paper.

Because of the dynamic nature of the Internet, any web addresses or links contained in this book may have changed since publication and may no longer be valid. The views expressed in this work are solely those of the author and do not necessarily reflect the views of the publisher, and the publisher hereby disclaims any responsibility for them.

Scripture quotations marked KJV are from the Holy Bible, King James Version (Authorized Version). First published in 1611. Quoted from the KJV Classic Reference Bible, Copyright © 1983 by The Zondervan Corporation.

Contents

This is a faithful saying, and worthy of all acceptation, that Christ Jesus came into the world to save sinners; of whom I am chief.[1]

1 Timothy 1:15

---

[1]   The Holy Bible, World Bible Publishers, King James Version, 1986.

High Priest

We have a High Priest,
Which cannot be touched,
He was tempted, yet without sin,
Come boldly,
Obtain mercy,
Find grace,
Do not wallow in sin,
Repent with godly sorrow,
Ask God for help,
Come on up,
Take Him at His word.
Amen.

Untitled

Seek God with all your heart.
My soul shall make her boast in the Lord.
My mind is moving forward,
Forgetting those things which are behind.
Seek and you will find,
The God of mercy and of Truth.
Do not be deceived,
God is not mocked,
Sow and you will reap,
Good and bad will repeat.

Your Face

Looking at your face I see my ancestors,
The pain, hurt, shame,
Is ever present today as it was yesterday.
Only God can save me from this world.
They prayed and believed,
They sang and moaned,
They wept and rejoiced,
Then God took them home.

I am Beauty

I am beauty,
I am love,
I am sent from up above.
I am the daughter, in whom God is well pleased,
I am young, powerful and will succeed.
In everything that I put my hands to do,
It is God's promise, not a distorted view.
I am fearfully and wonderfully made,
I am beauty wrapped up in grace.

Until It's Time

Until it's time,
I will do what you want.
Until it's time,
I will serve you.
Just don't leave me,
Don't go too far,
Until it's time.

After Effects

I do not like who you are,
Evil will come against you,
You will pay for what you do,
Vengeance is God's and you will repay,
I pity your soul, that longs for eternal damnation,
Hell requires your presence,
I am glad I am not following you,
Repent, ask for forgiveness and just maybe your burden will lighten,
If not, everything you attempt will fail,
You will not prosper and are in essence telling your soul to go to hell,
You are not protected, evil follows you and death is not far behind,
Suffer the little children, whose soul God shall find,
Can't you see what you've done?
Anger, bitterness, resentment,
Tired of being tired and sick,
Not that it matters as much as being filled with,
The Holy Spirit, will test me and see if there is any wicked way.
My God, why me?
Pardon my sins, hear my plea,
Take this burden, lighten my load,
Clean me up, make me white as snow.

Set the Standard

Set the standard,
For those who have given up on themselves and how they look,
Looks are not that important,
Oh, but they are,
See, 'cause when I put on my stilettos,
I literally stand above the rest,
My back arches perfectly,
I stand tall and proud,
Taking control of every ground,
I walk on.
Set the standard,
Show them how it is done,
High heels, stilettos,
Makeup flawless, hair done,
No one can compare.

Runway, not Basketball Dreams

Basketball, do you play?
That was the million dollar question,
I am tall, but I don't play basketball,
I do like to compete, but my court is the runway.
I love dressing up, with my high heels on,
My hair done and did,
Ready for the cat walk,
My mission and goal is to always win,
Just not on a basketball court.
That was not in The Plan.

Stones of Faith

Another page, this actually could have ended another chapter in this,
My story on the way to glory,
Trying to make history while I am here on this journey.
God, Jesus, the weight of your Glory,
How many pounds or tons of it,
So I can calculate how much therapy I will need and start saving for
the sessions;
But they are free with You,
So I will continue to write and hope to make a profit off this lot in life,
I have been given, but if I had it easy and were rich,
My life really would not have that much substance,
Therefore, I would also lack faith and in things hoped for and would
have no evidence of,
How I received the things You have for me,
Continue to bless me, God, and forgive me,
For the times I got angry at You for giving me this life,
Because it could be a lot worse,
So I walk on these stones of faith not knowing where I am going,
Because I cannot see the way, following a cloud by day and a pillar
of fire by night,
I am guided by the One who sent me and showed me the way of the
Master and,
How to follow what I am after, carefully seeking Him, and not him
with the biceps and triceps, and six pack,

Because he was not the one God ordered for me, but the one my fleshly eyes just happened to be,

Looking that way and I tripped and fell,

Losing track of God's time, getting on another road that is filled with quicksand and,

I am sinking,

I got to get back up because I was walking by faith on stones that were leading me to my destiny and purpose in life.

Untouchable

I am working on my poet game, motivated to improve my performance
and presentation,
Is going to be awesome,
I already know my stuff is going to be on point and chain ballin',
Making up words because there are none for my gift,
That will sift yours as wheat, so don't compare just be there,
To witness this moment in time that you will never get back, because
I am that,
Untouchable.

I Need Thee

I need Thee,
Feed me until I hunger and thirst no more.
Wrap me in Your arms and do not let go,
Come inside and make me whole,
I need thee.
Read me and let me see Your Glory,
Beyond the veil is where I beheld Your face,
And received strength to continue this race,
I must endure, not swiftly or in my own strength.
It is in the Lord that I must be strong, in the power of His might,
I take flight, soaring on wings of eagles,
With focus, I notice my need for You.

Open Mic Night

In the beginning was the Word.
I heard you,
Spoke to my spirit and soul,
Only a gift from God could do that.
It was Element.

Under Pressure

Resting in Him,
I cannot see what is going on,
I am in a cocoon and everybody can see this ball of string unraveling;
Being molded and shaped, fashioned so gently,
Chaos inside that is not so pretty,
Under pressure.

None Shall Touch Me

More time with You is what is needed for me,
To survive this set aside time,
For restoration and refreshing of my soul and spirit.
It is serious, I cannot do this alone.
A thousand at my right, ten thousand at my left,
But none shall touch me.

I Am Wins

Where did you go wrong,
Who told you, you were strong enough,
This life is not a game to be played,
Like Monopoly,
You could lose everything,
Without trusting me,
In the beginning was the Word,
In the middle you have a choice,
In the end, I Am wins.

Still Standing

I am up, literally up, spiritually up,
Standing on a firm foundation and not shaken,
By circumstances and situations,
That come up or arise out of the ground,
From no where, wandering around,
The opposition is so intense that,
I almost think I cannot handle this.

Ready to Fight

The amount of opposition I have been experiencing has been ludicrous,

It has been insane in the membrane,

I have been like, "Don't push me 'cause I am close to the edge, I'm trying not to lose my head, It's like a jungle sometimes it makes me wonder,

But God will have the final say on this one.

I give Him all the Glory, for blessing me with this opportunity,

To spread His Word and stomp on Satan's head,

I had to start my own fight club,

To become a member, you first of all have to be a child of God,

Accepting Jesus Christ as your Savior,

You must put on the whole Armor of God that you may be able to withstand the wiles of the devil,

You cannot become weary in well doing, because in due season you shall reap if you faint not,

And your flesh has to die, so the light of Christ can shine bright within you.

Then you are ready to fight,

Ready to conquer,

Prepared to pursue, overtake and recover it all.

Yes, I had to do some growing up in this season.

I do not wear pull-ups, but I believe I am a big girl now.

Predestined

Known haters,
Friend betrayers,
Caught up in this world of false investigators,
Looking for me to screw up,
For that right opportunity,
For them to catch me in their web of mistaken identity,
But it will give me the chance to tell them about my King,
Jesus said His Gospel would be preached to all nations around the
world,
Even if authorities are providing me with a stage,
A platform to preach, and what, teach,
And spread the Word of the Lord, Jesus Christ,
Regardless, it must be done, will be done,
Predestined already,
It's in God's plan,
Cannot change that.

Trust God

Getting over love lost, professor woes,
Money coming, future plans,
God demands,
Your time and commitment,
Summer school's about to finish,
Finding permanent work never ends.
Wishing for stability,
Health issues triggered by bitterness,
Removing sin, feeling helpless but not hopeless.
Having faith in things unseen,
Pushes me more to pursue my dreams.
Life is not a crystal stair,
Do not give up,
I will get there.
Trust God and hold on.

Expressions

Expressions,
Some like them, some don't.
I say what's on my mind,
In order to speed up the time,
Of understanding this chaos I am in,
Unfortunate, misfortune,
Will work for food and money,
But I do not have a sign,
Just experience and time to give,
Everybody is prospering but me,
Slowly I climb or walk or crawl rather,
My way through this muck and mire,
Feels like quick sand with people trying to pull me down,
Put me down, stomp me down,
I work hard for the money that I haven't seen the fruits of,
My labor is not in vain,
Believe Him,
Because His promises are yes and Amen.

Pressing

I thank You for providing for me in these times of,
I need to feed my spirit and soul,
So I read to probe,
Hoping to find an answer,
A Word that will encourage and serve its purpose,
To fulfill a prophecy.
My destiny is not to stay here,
But be elevated by you.
It feels like I am slowly progressing,
Pressing.

Great Reward

My great reward is coming,

If I would just hold on and endure until the end.

And this one will be happily ever after, in Jesus' name,

I rise, take up my bed and walk into my God-given destiny.

Peace and joy are mine because I abide under the shadow of the Almighty,

Who saved me from the pit of hell by giving His Son because of those who fell from grace due to their sins.

Because He Lives

God save me from bill collectors and,
Soulish haters hovering over me like I am dead meat,
Rotting about to die, but I live because He lives in me,
Shining like a star, yet a light seen from afar,
Catching the eye of many who come to see,
Who He is in me and why they cannot touch His deity,
Because He is God, He is, I Am,
Everything to me, my peace, joy, my liberty,
I am free indeed, because the Son has set it up that way.

Thirty-seven

Ten minutes to cherish thirty-seven,
Ode to this number,
Kind of glad it will be gone, I guess.
Wisdom learned, pain that burns,
A New Year and number,
Looking forward to obtaining more grace,
I love you, God.
Ode to this number, thirty-seven.

By Invitation Only

Come in, have a seat at my table,
And experience the life that has given me the label of,
Troublemaker, fornicator, famous hater (of the game).
The devil got me hemmed up so that I cannot breathe 'cause if I do,
I will smell death and destruction,
Nothing but an eruption of consequences with my name on them,
Scarred face from life's punches, beat down twice by,
Jail's function is not to rehabilitate, but to enhance the state of mind
I am already in,
So this is the menu that was prepared for me,
Flavors and tastes ever so enticing,
And now you are caught up, because you had a seat that was by
invitation only.

Just Sayin'

I am just sayin',
You cannot expect me to bow down and kiss your feet,
Because I am Queen and I will be a Queen when you leave.
Here are your exit papers,
I am just sayin',
Do not come to me expecting a perfect friend,
When your soul got holes in it,
Because of your trifling trends.
I am just sayin',
Do not try to use me or take advantage of my nice-ness and kindness,
Because on the other side is a devil waiting to cause trouble.
I am just sayin'.

This is Life

Deferred dreams, half eaten peas on a plate full of stuff that I do not like,
This is life.
Frustrated and also hated by unknown spirits who don't stop 'because they can't get enough,
Of breaking you down, making life miserable,
So you are looking for clowns to make you laugh to keep from crying,
Because you are tired of fighting, swinging low, low, low,
Missing marks, falling for the same old same old thing.
This is life.

Successful, Ambitious Woman

I am the successful, ambitious woman that lives on purpose, to complete the picture of the American Dream,
Which is C.R.E.A.M. – Cash Rules Everything Around Me,
Dollar, dollar bills with males that will let you settle for less than what you deserve,
Riding women's coattails because they too lazy to pursue what is rightfully theirs,
Caught up on stares and whispers of those who wear white sheets at knight,
Devising plans that can break our men down,
Leaving them with no sound, no voice,
So they cry out in secret places of jail cells and graves,
Going back to caves, crawling on the streets while their women hold it down,
Standing tall, taking licks from white and black and never falling down or losing her crown of,
Queen, she is the epitome of beauty that other cultures envy,
Successful, ambitious woman,
That, I am she.

Graduation Day

It is 2 a.m. and I am ready to graduate,
Preparing for this next plate of unknown dishes and wishes,
I forgot I made and prayed for the wrong darn thing, again.
I am ready to participate in life now,
I held it down while taking abuse,
God, where, oh, where has the time gone,
I missed beginning and it hurt until I was sick to my stomach from it,
And me disgustingly accepting foolish fiends who take pretty women's dreams,
When they are done doing their business, they throw them away as refuse,
Trash day is not until Sunday,
But you don't have to wait until then to have your mess dumped,
You can do it right now,
Before Graduation Day.

Reach, Grab, Pull

Your destiny is waiting for you,
Behold, I stand at the door and knock,
All you have to do is open it,
Reach out your hand,
Grab the door knob,
Pull the door open.
You did have to do a little work,
But not that much because once you were open, you became free.
I became free to live, rule and reign in you life and show you what
you missed twice,
Then give it back to you 30, 60, and 100 fold.
Reach, grab, and pull,
Your destiny is waiting for you.

Dreams and Steel Beams

Dreams and steel beams holding me up,
When I am feeling kind of down,
Life is filled with so much uncertainty,
It is hurting me that I cannot see the path I am on or why I am on it,
Will I understand it better by and by,
Lord, when is the morning coming,
Because it's been night time for about 30 years,
Filled with tears and fears and me building walls with limited access,
My heart being auctioned off without my permission,
My dreams and steel beams are holding me up as I stop and strike
a pose,
Standing still so no one will see me breathe-ing,
I am not here, but God's spirit is in me and demons see clearly,
Through the spiritual fog and mist,
As so not to be tricked into missing their appointments to kill, steal
and destroy my dreams and steel beams that are holding me up.

Waiting for Permission

See, I want to be having lunch in downtown Salt Lake City,

Taking trips to Italy, it is that I envy, at times, the lives of those who actually have one,

While mine is being prepared, created through heartache and stress from haters and game players,

I want to be strolling on Route 66, just because I can or I got it like that,

I don't, so I press through the process and this mess that smells,

But it is cleaning me up, producing character that is sweet and mmm...good,

I am tasting my destiny, walking by faith,

Patience is a virtue...whatever that means,

I must have needed it real bad, because I keep on taking that test over and over and over,

Until I pass and the Lord gives me permission to have lunch, in Salt Lake and Italy.

Freedom Writer

What made me start writing?
Honestly, it was the hurt of daddy's gone and mama's home and I
was about to get that whippin' she's been waiting to give me all day.
I write to release my journey to excellence,
Ain't been easy, I got a little queasy at times on this roller coaster
called life,
And it is not a game, so you gotta' make the right move and stay in
line with the Master, as your leader.
Following Him will lead you to right-ness, wholeness and,
Freedom, Writer I am.

New Journal

New Journal, holla'! New Journey, Father!

Help me,

I can't do it without You,

Ink to paper,

I call on You, with my words requesting Your presence,

Needing Your guidance as You take me higher,

I am learning to search my soul while You are filling me with Your Spirit,

Cleansing, purifying I am getting burned only because I haven't died yet,

To myself, otherwise I would not feel a thing,

So why am I trippin'?

Die to self,

To be elevated and helped.

My Identity

I Define You.
Your definition is in Me.
In me you live, move and have your being.
It is only in Me.
Without Me ye can do nothing,
Everything comes back to Me.
Stop the pity party and start the praise party,
You won!
You have the victory, in Me and with Me.
My definition is in Christ.
I am complete in Christ.

Help

How do I get there, God?
Take me, Lord.
I believe,
I see,
I need Thee.
Help me,
Feed me.
Open my Word to see Me.

Hard Places

I am trying to maintain my composure as best I can,
Barely "keeping up appearances",
Lost my sight, can't promote like I want,
Rent due, car payment late,
I need help, God,
Wrong job, back to old one,
In between jobs, in between loves,
Not here, nor there,
Wondering when my time will come,
My change is going to come,
I accomplished that, yes,
Still blessed and in mess,
Waiting for God to speak for me,
Redeem me, please God,
I ask for more help,
I ask for your help, God,
Fix me, help me, heal me, deliver me,
God please, I am pleading,
But I guess You are walking with me,
I am being carried up and up,
Away, like in the movies, but stuck here choosing wrong directions,
Seeking leading from my Father,
Trying to listen as Satan tries to kill me softly with his words,
Killing me softly with his words, telling my whole life as lies,
I am wiser and stronger because of you, Satan,
I bounce back and get up walking tall because Jesus died and won
it all,

It is finished, I have the victory,

I just need to see and be and let God arise and my enemies be scattered,

Work it out, God, remove the chatter and let me hear you,

Flow in me, in my heart,

Let me hear you blow and sound the alarm,

It is time to wake up and be heard,

Decree and declare my Word, says the Lord,

Begin to shake things up with the voice I have given you,

Wake up sleeper, arise from death,

Be born again and receive my help,

Bless me indeed for my spirit is willing, but flesh is weak,

So I need the Father, Son, and Holy One,

Holy Ghost, reappear and grab hold of my soul to keep me,

Breathe in my life, eternal working wonders like bread from heaven,

My manna in the morning, like dew,

I receive you fresh anointing,

I am wanting more and more of You, God,

As I go through hard places, feeling stuck and crying like I am,

Because I am dying more and more to be like You,

Making this little light of mine shine, shine, shine,

On me, let the light from the lighthouse shine on me, please.

Born Again

Twelve years young receiving Christ as one,
Being baptized with a friend, we have in Jesus to the end,
Hearing the message on one bright and sunny day,
Moved to go down by invitation, one way,
No more sermons to pierce our heart and souls,
It was time to confess and believe what God did,
Clearly remembering, my now forgotten sins.

Untitled

Suffering is not meaningless, rejoice in them always,
Your labor is not in vain, Jesus bore our pains,
You now have character, for the purpose of which God created,
Ultimately revealed in due time, you will be glad you waited,
He came that we might have life and even more abundantly,
Help me carry the cross of great pain and suffering,
It is not meaningless, but will serve its purpose,
What kind of season is this?
Freakin' frustration, trying to hold my peace,
Unfair people that don't give, but take,
All they can from you to fulfill their self prophecies,
I have never been around so many selfish props, please,
I am included in that category, but not at this moment,
It sucks to the third power, maybe to the tenth,
But it's not about me, I keep forgetting this,
Talking about folks from on high,
All caught up in the flesh, allowing spirits to take flight,
Just preach the Gospel, the Holy Spirit will convict,
And move sinners toward true, authentic repentance,
Is there another me in Rome, can I switch places right quick?
I need a moment or two, just until this is over, then,
I am through, not polished or purified, frustrated and tired,
Beat down, knocked over, spit on and fired,
Still strong and standing, hurting every time,
Never use to cruel and unusual punishment, that penalty should be
a fine,
Do not let it become an expectation, press on through,
Put on the whole armor, make it a part of you.

Mentality

Not liking seasons and circumstances, taking chances,
In time you will change into a new creation,
Behold all new things in Christ,
Old things have passed away,
Begin to change your mentality,
Change your mentality,
Chain your mentality, take every thought into captivity,
Bringing them into submission,
Your mindset is key to buildings that stand,
Because of a Cornerstone that exists,
Dying to live again and bring life to all men,
I am building you up, sending you out as sheep.

Relentless

Time out for playing games,
The enemy is working overtime,
Killing, stealing and destroying nations,
Attacking the Kingdom of God,
Leaving wounded soldiers, bleeding trying to recover-it all,
Depends on the faith of the believer,
Don't believe the report of the deceiver,
Be relentless in your pursuit of the promises of God-,
Is interceding on your behalf, He is for you,
Remember, we have the victory,
Jesus paid it all,
It is finished.

139

God knows.

He knows me.

He knows when I sit down and when I rise up,

He discerns my thoughts from afar,

He searches out my path and my lying down and is acquainted with all my ways,

Even before a word is on my tongue,

God knows it altogether.

Nickel and Dimed

Nickel and dimed,
Running out of time,
Brotha's got an agenda,
He is not on mine,
Two parties going their separate ways,
Trying to make paper,
Flat.

Thirty-Nine

Thirty-nine and looking fine.
My, my, my where has the time,
Gone, it is, along with my youth,
Looking back at stiletto days,
Switching fast and making haste,
As not to be left behind by the world's pace,
Thirty-nine and wouldn't take nothing back,
Because wisdom's crown looks better than the world's fool hat.

Little Boxes

Fair-weather woman,
People will try to put you into their little boxes,
Like foxes in holes that have no place to lay their head,
At night, staying up trying to live up to standards that bust,
Because you felt obligated to fit on a side you were not suppose to.
The pressure was thick and almost overwhelming until I gained
understanding,
That I did not have to do anything or answer to anyone, but God,
I did not have to go there; I did not have to be there,
Things going on that you know not of,
Dealing with issues and currents that make you lose focus.
God is in control of you, He guides and He leads,
No condemnation is freeing for believers who don't have little boxes
to deal with.

Prayer 2.16

I will bless the Lord at times; His praise shall continually be in my mouth,

My soul shall make her boast in the Lord, the humble shall here thereof and be glad,

Oh magnify the Lord with me and let us exalt His name together because,

Last night I was enveloped and surrounded by the enemy, trying to get at me and make words come out that were not sanctified, just, or holy,

So let me bless the Lord and give Him praise, all the time and in times of trouble and despair,

When it seems like no one really cares, but stare at you wondering and frustrated that you are not their puppet to string up and down and jump when they say;

Sick and tired of folks with wrong spirits and tendencies that serve their own needs adding to church doctrines like false prophets with hidden agendas to get your money, your time and your mind,

Jesus, help us to do justly, to love mercy, and walk humbly with You,

Let me fulfill these deeds and not others needs pushed and pressed upon me, In Jesus' name, Amen.

Coming Together

Coming together, my outlook on life is looking better and better,
I go day to day praying to God to make a way for me in this wilderness
valley of death,
Working on dreams, writing down visions given to me,
Ordered in the beginning, before my mother knew me,
I believed in myself, looking to God for help,
I see no end to my success if I walk by faith, on water looking to Jesus,
I won't fall or fail, victory is guaranteed,
It is all coming together,
My outlook on life is looking better and better.

No Praise

No praise,
Do lift me up, no praise wanted here,
The Savior paid the price for all the praise,
Paying the price for you and me,
Giving us words to say, to bless Him,
No praise wanted here.

80/ 20

Tired of trifling Negroes, trying to be heroes in disguise and are really zeroes,
Being exposed by me because I have been there and done that,
Bought a t-shirt with that game on it,
Now you want to jump on it without a ring and a contract,
That is binding; your time is winding up, slowly aging,
No longer eye candy, but fat Randy whose card has been punched;
Now you want an 80, but all you are left with is 20's,
Because 80 knows she can do better and bad all by herself;
Created as queen, a mystery to thieves who try to steal her stuff,
She waits diligently and patiently, finding solace in the Almighty God,
Prince of Peace, Wonderful Counselor, Everlasting King of Glory,
I have been groomed for the best and will not settle for less,
So keep your sorry's, because you will never ever touch this glory!

Untitled

Lilies and green grass,
An antithesis from the past,
Serpents and lions being trampled upon,
Trees with apples that are now gone.

Waiting for Next

Books are in me, trying to get them out one by one,
Help me, ready for businesses to begin booming,
Waiting for next, can't see walking blindly,
Seeing loves, what I miss,
Wrong dudes, hill street blues,
Got to get over shady, shiesty fools,
Wrong suitors, not my preference,
Pick and choose,
Checking references, looking for God's love,
Wanted bachelor, BMW (Black Man Working), fully loaded,
With God and Christ and most of all the Holy Ghost.

Nightmares

Books on tape, lies on file,
Working my nerves, all the while,
Getting your fix, depleting my soul,
Like vampires thirsty, leprechaun's gold.
You need this, I want that,
Deeper issues, go way back,
Before we met.
Got me twisted, mixed up in mess,
I told Jesus and He rescued me from hell's fiery furnace,
And that darn burn notice.
Asked for wisdom, God gives liberally,
To prevent nightmares from the beginning.

State of Play

State of mind, state of play,
I don't know what will happen today,
Devil's plans, unrighteous hands,
A dangerous thing,
Waiting for those who trust in God,
To cave in and join the blind side.

Bethesda

Mentally tired, soul is drained,
Waiting for God to trouble His fountain,
And make me whole again,
To renew my spirit.

M.I.A.

False Daddy's, foxy ladies,
Living just enough for the themselves,
Forgetting the cares of,
Growing up, souls undone,
Looking for authority, finding none.

My Psalm

God is my Shepherd, He lets me rest,
He leads me to quiet pools that are pretty and fresh,
He gives me new strength and guides me to right paths,
He is with me and protects me and prepares a nice spread,
Of blessings and favor, welcoming me as an honored guest,
God fills my cup, all the way to the brim,
His goodness and love, with me as long as I live,
This is my Psalm.

Untitled

Thanks for the compliment, you sly dog;
I need your help,
Hidden agendas, lady's frail,
You are not for me;
But thanks for the compliment, crafty soldier,
Your title has scorned me into disbelief and disarray,
Wondering why you are in the enemy's parade,
Disguised as the anointed one, perpetrating as a false son of a,
God that is your idol and down fall,
Gotta get you help, intercede for your sins.

False Prophets

False prophets, court dockets,
That reveals the truth of the matter;
Your life is an open book, but I am reading between the lines and,
I don't like what I see;
Rewrite that chapter because I don't want to be in it,
Editing done, sin repeated,
Forgiveness comes, after repentance.
Single ladies, others hating,
Schemes to get closer to you,
Out of darkness into His marvelous light,
But you are caught up, tied to a burning bed,
Nothing is said to release you from bondage,
Help is close by, written on correspondence from God's book of promises,
Designed to prosper you and guide you into all truth and provide proof of your redemption from sin.
Paradox being formed with every step you take in,
Prosperity waiting on your right actions and obedience to the Father;
Deliver us from evil sanctions,
If this is a man's world, watch out girls from those ones that prey,
Watching for weaknesses, not seen in your esteem,
Everyone is a suspect, like false prophets and real ones too.

Final Scene

Not liking you right now,
Disappearing acts are final.
You are now just a memory and forever will be,
Cast into the forgetfulness sea.
Forgiveness is mandatory, no timeframes attached,
Want to wait until the rapture or until Jesus comes back,
This is unknown, actions must be made now,
Before the final ending,
Completing the scene.
Cut.

Book Material

What a sorry excuse for an hū-,
Man you should not even have that title, to say the least,
Thank you for the material; you are a class act,
Not too many like you, crazy, no love,
Destructive behavior, driving away normal,
Stuck in small worlds, criminal mind,
Pathetic, pity, small, minūte, period.
I feel better already. Book number three.
The beginning.

Be Wary

Watch over our eyes; make sure they do not wander into the next man's life,

Ruining homes, changing tones, breaking ships that precede relation,

Keep me focused, don't want to notice your closet marked with skeletal bones,

Missing graveyards and their proper homes,

Shaken up by open invitations, led astray by charismatic notations;

Buyer beware of property currently owned,

Wrong games played, last bet stays until you pay the penalty for making that choice.

God's Grace

By Your grace I am in this place,

Learning lessons in this Christian race,

Accelerated spiritual classes, Master's passes, V.I.P. notices, not for novices,

Still on milk, needing solid spiritual food that can be chewed and pondered on,

Yesterday is gone, cannot accept returns or refunds on used items,

Background checks tell your entire story,

Good and bad and yes, the ugly,

Tell me why I am here right now,

To fulfill a prophecy and reveal God's promise,

To bring me prosperity, and hope God has not forgotten.

By God's grace, I am in this place.

Moving Up

I am about to move on up into the Glory side, into a deluxe apartment
home,
Moving on up, no longer stuck on pause,
God has pushed play and fast forwarded me into Redemption,
Time has been redeemed,
I am cashing in on blessings and promises guaranteed,
Inheritance paid by my friend who sticks closer than a brother,
Moving on up, I was last,
But now the first shall be and will be,
God is able to bring to pass all that you thought was lost,
Redeeming the time, taking back stolen property and then some,
OMGoodness, this is way too much,
Exceedingly and abundantly, blessings coming through windows of
heaven,
Making room to receive this heavenly treasure,
God is redeeming the time and I am moving on up.

Waiting

Been around the block and I can't find my baby,
I don't know why he has gone away,
I don't know where he could be, I can't find my baby,
It is because you have been looking for love in all the wrong places,
Clubs, bowling alleys, where you find stray cats and dogs with no Master,
Sometimes plastered, not knowing who you are or whose you are,
Lost, and your first love is waiting and longing for your return to Him,
This relationship is a need, filling holes you tried to cover with lust,
Neglecting to flee, you strayed farther and farther away,
Sinking deep in sin, far from the peaceful shore,
Where your first love is waiting for your return,
Longing to be with you, loving you regardless,
Come unto Me, I am waiting.

Secrets in the Heart

Losing friends – girl friend betrayal,
Mixed with heart failures,
Good girls gone bad,
Losing track, changing hands,
I stole his eyes,
Lies deep within,
Suppression is oppression,
Good girls with bad impressions,
Secrets in the heart,
Sadness in the dark.

Summer and Winter

Friends for a season,
That lasted too long,
Now the season is gone,
Lasting impressions sown,
Missing affirmations unknown,
Consistent talks and regular walks,
That was summertime,
This is winter.
Birthday celebrations, family relations,
Joyful season, given for a reason,
It accomplished its intent,
That was summertime,
This is winter.

Wicked Sinners, Gospel Killers

Wicked sinners, Gospel killers,
Preying on children that are God's,
Roaming around, seeking the found,
Looking back, from day to day,
Trying to keep my soul out of harm's way.
Despondent looks, spiritual crooks,
Taken over by Satan's hook.
Soon they will be cut off,
Wishing they had not paid the cost.
God is laughing, at the wicked,
Those who don't seek repentance.
The destiny of the wicked is doom and gloom,
Eventually ending up in Satan's pool.
Time is quickly running out,
God will come to redeem the devout.
The righteous will soon receive their crown,
For winning the race on this wicked ground.

Who is Like God

Who is like God,
I certainly am not,
I have this name that means a lot,
French derivatives that have various meanings,
Often describing characters,
That is lacking and not beaming.
God is like no one,
I Am the alter,
He is only and one,
Who is like God, it is only His Son.

Published and Exposed

Inspired by hurt,
That has to be released,
Published and exposed,
To meet a need,
I got good news, released after the bad,
Published and exposed, releasing the mad.

The Truth

If you think you are lonely now, wait until the rapture comes,
One will be taken; the other will be left,
To fend off spirits, seeking to consume them to death.
Sinners will be looking for someone to cool their tongues,
They made the choice, now there is none.
The Truth was here.

Chief of Sinners

Chief of Sinners,
No good thing dwells within me,
I am the chief of infidelity.
Rotten to the bone, of filthy lucre,
Sinful natures eventually exposed.
Chief of Sinners is everyone's title,
Perjury, adultery, these are the writer's,
For all have sinned and fallen short,
No one is exempt from becoming chief of this sort.

Unsuccessful Robbers

Subtle fears of increased, intense attacks from the enemy,
Following me like I got hidden treasures, I do.
Visions of my destiny make them work harder,
Energized by principalities and powers,
Trying to steal and kill assignments before they are complete,
These are unsuccessful robbers.

Intimidating Love

Intimidating on paper, threatened by the presence,
Your insecurities revealed through guilty pleasures of,
Backbiting, sarcasm and other dirty tricks,
You will reap what you sow, eventually falling into a ditch.
Love the Lord with all your heart, soul and mind,
This is the first commandment that will allow you to hit rewind.
Love your neighbor as yourself and you will no longer be blinded,
By the ignorance that has attached itself to you,
Love is the word that covers sins' multitude.

Playground

Sorry suckers, different mothers,
Christian homes and broken bones,
Church is a playground, full of dolls and soldiers,
Games of life and sorry, fill the foyers.
People searching for perfect love,
Blinded by hurts, pains, and perfect curves.
Damaged spirits, sorrowful souls,
Locked in cages, the key no one holds.

Nineteen Eighty-four

Being spied on like a criminal,
Artificial intelligence is invisible,
Feeling like Big Brother is out of control,
Like peeping toms on patrol,
Need to have eyes in the back of my head,
So as not to let the enemy creep in,
In bed, fighting off spirits who invited themselves in,
Rude and unruly suckers within,
Israel is under attack; Jesus is on His way back,
Coming in slow motion,
To allow prophecies take over and over,
We are experiencing the same thing,
The devil has no new tricks,
Always playing the same game,
In that day, you will be spied on like criminals,
Artificial intelligence will be invisible,
Big brother will be out of control,
Peeping toms will be on patrol.

What I Write About

I don't write about perfect lilies and trees,

Green pastures that are freeing,

Colors of the rainbow that can bring some folks joy,

I write about relationships gone bad,

And some that left me sad,

With bad taste in my mouth, thinking I wasted a whole lot of time,

Making me wait, putting me on their schedule,

With appointments that were not level playing,

I write about workers with bad spirits,

Seeking to kill and destroy mine,

Like we are on a battlefield behind enemy lines,

I can't see the cross; everything I see is false,

It almost made me crazy,

A thin line between love and insanity,

Not about to plea another false statement,

Sentenced to life, I was saved by Jesus,

You see He freed us, and now we have the victory,

But I must continue to fight and write about this,

It's like hit or miss when you serve Him,

I write about me on journeys,

Trying to save lost stories,

Putting things on paper,

That may lose my favor,

But it's ok and better to please God and not man,

Poems written according to,

God's will be done on earth as it is in heaven,

My poems are saturated with love and hatred,

Against people's spirits and experiences,
That have brought me low enough to actually see and be in the midst
of Christ,
I believe I may have been in that temple Isaiah spoke about,
Where God's train had filled it out,
I came out glowing and knowing who I was and whose I was,
So I could write about it.

Resolution

January bring new beginnings, the year is twenty-thirteen,
February bring me favor and things that are not seen,
March bring me mercy that I shall forever obtain,
April bring Almighty God that I might bless His Holy name,
May bring me Your might and include with this Your power,
June bring me the Lord Jesus, every day and every hour,
July that I may know You are my Jehovah Jireh,
August bring beauty for ashes, my crown in the last hour,
September make unto Him sacrifices of a pleasing scent and aroma,
October birthing greatness and opportunity becoming closer to my
lover,
November bring Good News, spreading the Gospel is key,
December reveal my destiny and purpose, back to new beginnings.

At This Age

Help me to be content and not focus on the not haves,
I am blessed beyond measure, no reason to be sad,
Help me to love like you do and forgive many times over,
All the hurts and wrongs, this let me not remember,
Give me wisdom and discernment,
For better decisions and fewer mistakes,
Give me grace to sustain and Your favor I will gladly take,
For all that You have done God, I thank You for Your Son,
All that You have given me, your promises are forever won,
I am blessed and will bless you at all times of the day,
At this age, I will do this, your name is worthy of all praise,
What I want at this age is to be thankful for my needs,
Being met and predestined and victory guaranteed,
I thank you God, at this age.

Fresh Pages

Fresh pages to start again,
A life's journey, Satan tried to end too soon,
Still standing on God's Word,
His promises keep me going day to day,
Increasing my faith, by priests being heard,
Fresh pages, ink loves to touch,
Symbolizing a relationship,
Kindled by desire, fire and a gift from above,
This is my destiny, starting again and again,
Telling new stories from beginning to end,
Fresh pages to start again,
A life's journey Satan tried to end.

Impetus

Gotta' pray more and worship more,
Due to crazies, can't stand them,
Gaining momentum with each day,
They pass, while I am saying bye-bye,
You do not have my peace no more, no more,
No more, hit the road, Zack,
And don't you come back,
You're building me up, while I am pushing you down,
Underground, into the abyss of hell where you belong,
My God has not forsaken me, but He is praying for me,
Carrying me through the valley of the shadow of death and,
I fear no evil because my God is with me,
Caring for me with his everlasting love and arms hiding me,
Under His shadow I am safe from harm's way,
I gotta' let go of the bitterness to be a better witness in this day,
Professing Jesus, the Way, Truth and Life,
You gotta' go through Him to get to me.

Betrayal

Sick and tired of being betrayed, trapped insanity pleas for false help,

Wolves cry for nothing, trying to bate you just to rape you,

Taking things you thought hidden, but the enemy saw a way in,

Selfless being, the chief master of this sin,

Crossing lines that define life, this is what strife is,

All I go through to become gold,

Fire purifies the deepest soul,

Those too shallow cannot behold,

The goodness and fruit that will be produced,

By life's betrayal and its endless pursuit.

False Prophets, Court Dockets

Dealing with false prophets and other people's court dockets,
Crazy spirits, running rampant,
Looking for stable souls to dump on and take advantage of,
Depleting you and trying to suck the life out that God gave you,
Peace I receive, when I keep my mind on Him and not the false prophets,
Trying to get into my pockets or,
Court fools that try to drag you to jail with them.

Gaining Momentum

Gaining momentum, slaying dragons and lions with my bear hands,

Taking sand and throwing it in the enemy's eyes, blinding him,

Not knowing he is going into that chasm that God prepared,

No victory for you, should have stayed in the choir and followed God's direction,

Now it's too late, doom is waiting for your stare,

No time to waste, we both have things to do,

Our results will be different,

I win, you lose.

On Earth

Undergoing spiritual assault,
I cannot recognize the demons of this occult,
Looking around with spiritual eyes,
Seeking criminals in disguise,
Wolves in sheep's clothing can confuse slow believers,
Different game, same rules apply,
Man cannot live by bread alone,
But by every word that proceeds out of the most of the Most High,
God, I need you to move something,
God, I need you to do something,
My courage is under fire and my desires are being put on hold,
As I try to destroy these fools on the battlefield,
Not wrestling against flesh and blood,
But against principalities that are in my reality,
Making this game of life intense,
I cannot forget though,
How God delivered me back then and,
I heard stories of how He does it again and again,
Claiming victory after victory,
Up to the final day when,
He brings it all home,
On earth, as it is in Heaven.

Critical Condition

Fools following, Satan keeps calling,
Knocking on my door, I hit the floor,
Praying and worshiping my God,
Saying please deliver me and please set me free,
I am breaking chains, not feeling restrained,
Gaining energy and drive each and everyday,
I am pressing into God and coming out gold.

The Plan

I can't even explain it,
This season I'm in now,
It is outrageous,
Remuneration bursting out of the seams,
Able to live life like I never dreamed,
Man, God, wow, you really did this,
Bringing me in and through and out of miry pits,
All of the crying and tears and hurt and pain,
Was really nothing, but worth it,
Just to see this day,
I think I'm covered with so much oil,
I am on a new level,
Defeating lions and poisonous snakes,
Ready for new devils,
Yes, God, I know that you are not done,
With me the battle new has just begun,
I know you began this work,
And now it must be finished,
So continue to move me and use me,
Until it's done,
Walking on water, man, this is really nice,
I was an observer, but now I know what it is really like,
My eyes were focused on everything around me,
Not looking up to Jesus, I could not see,
He had me all the time,
Even before I moved,
I had to transform and renew the words that were in my mind,

Your real life is really played out in your midnight dreams,

God has a plan for you,

But you have to believe,

He will bring you prosperity and the future that you hope for,

Jeremiah 29:11 opened up the door.

Momentous Reward

I am gaining momentum God, because of you,

Satan is creeping and peeping, he's on the move,

Not knowing what is going down or coming in the future,

I am cautious when walking next to known villains,

Guarding my heart from people that try to kill, steal and destroy,

Every move up that infamous hill,

Wisdom, discernment have become my best friends,

Listening to them always,

I have become like Superwoman,

Using supernatural, God-given abilities,

To trample and pull down the Anti-Christ man,

God has given us these days to make sure we bring others to the Way,

Continue to move on, move up,

Pressing forward to get the ultimate crown,

That is our reward.

Christian Hustlers

Christian hustlers,
Words that don't even go together,
Seeing you coming a mile away,
Devious schemes are like child's play,
To you, I really do not matter,
As you try to get into my pockets,
To increase your platters,
Lenders, beware of these types of borrowers,
Give them a ride and they'll take you even farther than you wanted,
And then show off the merchandise they got from you,
'Cause you fell for their old sob story.
Anchors weigh down boats and so do Christian Hustlers.

Jesus Take This Wheel

Jesus take this wheel,
Because I am tired of driving,
Going in wrong directions,
Missing signs just to tickle my pleasure,
I cannot do this on my own,
Making choices that put me on hold,
Stuck in somebody else's fantasy,
Now realizing Plato's Allegory,
Living in my dreams,
While I let God lead me beside still waters,
He covers me, protects me,
Sitting on the passenger side,
While I let Him drive.

In That Day

Still dealing with devil fools,
But goodness and mercy continue to follow,
Weary at times, renewed by God on High,
Walking and not fainting, waiting on the Lord,
To destroy all enemies, be prepared to fight,
Every single day, wake up putting on God's Armor,
So as to quench the fiery darts ready to be aimed,
Satan gets high on planning evil attacks,
It's a drug to him, so he won't stop, can't stop,
That is his job,
To kill, steal and destroy,
So we must rise up as Lions of Judah,
Ready to fight and take back our lives,
The joy of the Lord is my strength,
Bow down and worship Him,
So He can restore your soul,
In that day has come.

Eliminated and Erased

Ex-'s trying to come back and get what they lost,
A day late and two dollars short,
Missed opportunities,
To be with God's honey,
Lost loves don't taste good,
Sour heads dwelling on could haves and should haves,
The time card has been punched,
Years to show up and step up,
Too many violations and citations,
Bruises and cuts,
Float on, sorry suckers,
Healing from damages to heart, soul and spirit,
Waiting for the day when you won't be in memory,
Eliminated and erased, and mostly replaced,
By a real man.

Life

Action packed notices, given on point,
References checked,
Words received, mandates given,
To exceed my expectations,
Going forth with renewed vigor and vitality,
Strengthened mentality,
God, I don't know what You are doing,
Whatever it is, please keep me,
Posted with life's movie trailers,
So that I can peak into the future,
And see what the enemy sees,
Attacking me with all kinds of artillery,
It ain't right, but gotta' fight,
Because of what Jesus did way back on Calvary,
He died for me and rose again,
That I might have life and,
Life more abundantly.

Covering

I can't hardly take it, can't even shake this,
On me, covering from the Holy One,
The only One that can save me,
Surrounded by warring and ministering angels,
To protect me from fiery darts,
It's a sweet anointing, like awning,
Shielding me from life's elements.

Crazy

Still dealing with crazy,
Man, they won't go away,
Trying to get better at not avoiding,
But showing more of God,
Because I *should* be more like Him,
Yet still a work in progress,
Mastering all kinds of tests at this level,
Didn't know it was going to be like this,
I would have missed out on precious blessings,
Not knowing the future would hold this,
God knew His plans for me,
But I could not see it,
Because I would not read it,
His Word opened my eyes and the doors and windows of heaven,
To pour out such blessings that I have not room enough to receive it,
Conceive it, perceive,
It blows my mind,
On cloud nine, with this whole experience,
Gotta' come down now and deal with crazy.

I See Me

I see me in the F-U-T-U-R-E,
I am ballin', why you keep on callin',
You didn't even know,
Three years ago my name was unknown,
Now the world knows me better than you,
You need to float on, float on,
Because this ship has sailed and left the pier,
On to new horizons, I am smizing,
Like Top Models, I am rising to whole new levels,
Squashing devils with my pinky finger,
It's that easy, because Jesus died, for my 'forgive me's,
Granting me access to all of His authority and power,
Yes, I see me in the F-U-T-U-R-E,
AND YOU ARE NOT THERE!

Falling Short

I seem to fall short these days,
People's expectations now a purple haze,
Too much pressure to perform in roles,
I did not sign up for those, but told you are,
As I fill in the blanks with words that are not mine,
The responsibility of it all continues to rise,
I want to turn in my resignation,
If only temporarily, just for a moment or season,
Maybe because I seem to fall short these days,
More than I care to.

As Christ Loves

As Christ loves the church,
So a man must love me,
Unconditionally and totally with no strings,
Keep it clean please,
Glorify God with me,
Highly exalted with me,
Seeking God continually together we will be,
Husbands love your wives just as Christ loved the church and gave
His life for it,
Guy friends, be encouraging to your female friends,
Don't just think about her skin,
Let this mind be in you which was also in Christ Jesus,
Yes, He loves us, He loved us,
So you must keep it clean from all unrighteousness,
He freed us, so grateful for the cross,
Here I am,
Please God send,
A church that loves me.

Your Name

The only way she would take your name,
And then speak your name is if you do not play games,
With her heart, making it an art,
To get to know her and be with her always,
Not caring what others think,
Because she takes care of you and satisfies your needs,
As if you were the only one in this world,
Just the two of us, would be the theme,
Living life abundantly, with each other,
Because she took your name and,
God blessed it.

Incompetence and Ignorance

Dealing with incompetence and ignorance,
People who judge and think that they are better than,
Because of the color of their skin,
It is a sin,
Not be black or white or brown,
But to hate is like murderers going to jail to find redemption,
Where there is none,
They get shunned by society,
Living in sobriety,
I feel like I need a drink sometimes,
But I must not be filled with wine,
So I ask the Holy Spirit to come in and dine,
With me and help me deal with incompetent and ignorant fools,
Who say there is no God, where is your God,
He is right here, waiting to say, you fool,
To raise you from the depths of your hell,
I can't even imagine what it is like to live in your mind,
Not really satisfied with yourself,
Projecting hate towards that which you cannot change,
My color, deranged thoughts,
That will not happen because,
The righteous are delivered and protected,
You have been arrested,
Charged with racism and discrimination,
It is only a matter of time,
Before you meet the real judge and Maker of you,
Incompetent and ignorant fool.

Corrected

Your game is weak,
Can't even speak, write,
Addressing ladies in lazy terms,
Like no home training,
Let me put you on pause,
As I walk into the room,
To correct you,
God raised a Queen,
Not to be controlled by fiends or players who love games,
Corrected, you are welcome,
Now available as your reference,
Not to be addressed as 'Hey' or 'You',
Losing all cool,
Points are gained by gentlemen with classy hats and suave demeanors,
Who address ladies correct and with respect,
Sending you back to school,
Because you did not pass the Gentlemen's Test,
Corrected, you are welcome,
Now available as your reference.

Second Chronicles

I need you, to constantly feed upon you and your Word,

To sustain me and keep me from falling,

Going in the wrong direction,

I must move forward, towards that prize,

I rise higher and higher,

Each day as I open my mouth,

Open my mouth and speak those things that be not,

As though they were in my life,

I must also cast down those master spirits,

Who are the world rulers of this present darkness,

And spirit forces of wickedness in the heavenly, supernatural sphere,

I am here, right now,

You got eyes on me,

But I clearly see your attempts and wicked demise,

To compromise my right standing with God,

I rest in His arms at night,

As He restores my soul from the attacks of the day,

Being prepared each moment,

To stand against all the strategies and deceits of the devil,

I am now mellow,

Keeping my composure, under extreme exposures of intense heat,

I come out unscathed or untouched,

Glowing and showing the enemy up,

Is what God does for a living,

Mine is not in vain,

No Cain destruction here, in my body,

The earth is calling,

Crying out with innocent blood,

It is now a flood,

Preparing the way for God to cleanse all unrighteousness,

And bring His Kingdom down here on earth,

These wars are just the beginning,

You ain't seen nothing yet,

It's about to be on and poppin',

In the spiritual realm, already happening with murders and killings,

Every hour of the day, we must pray for the nation,

Humble ourselves, seek God's face,

And then turn from our wicked ways,

So we can hear from Heaven and,

Be forgiven of our sins,

To have a healed land.

Relevance

Everything prevalent is not really relevant,
I am living not in a pleasant situation,
Wanting revelation of what to do next,
I am perplexed and speechless,
My thoughts need less scrutiny and more fruitful bearing,
Graces to stimulate my spirit man to love man always or unconditionally,
Without faults, finding their way back into the scene,
Take two of these and call me in the morning,
One, being God's Word as lamp unto your feet,
And a light unto your path,
Two, being prayer to be done with much supplication,
This is relevant and you are too,
Not the material things that tend to consume you.
Everything relevant is not really prevalent,
I must bear fruit, not find faults,
Read God's Word, pray and stop shopping,
It's irrelevant to the Great Commission,
My mission is not to find Gucci handbags or Chanel sunglasses,
Because they cause clashes between me and God,
These two masters who want to be served,
Require your services,
One bearing fruit and the other who knows what becomes of it,
Nothing much after living in bliss,
And missing an eternal wish to know Him.

Backside of the Desert

I am sitting on the backside of the desert,
Waiting for heaven to open,
And pour out all these blessings upon me,
I am on my knees, begging and pleading with God,
Jesus, help me please,
I get these visions that are a tease,
Like movie trailers,
Only a peak, to keep you going,
Coming soon to a theater near you,
Is me on top, soaring all the way to the moon,
It is going be like ice cream on a sunny day,
So sweet, being in God's favor this way,
But I was sitting on the backside of the desert,
Waiting for years, being processed and purified with lots of tears,
Now ready as gold,
All impurities gone,
The perfect movie is about to begin,
Starring me and Jesus, as God,
It is my life's story.

It's On

It's about to be on and poppin',
I am not stopping,
Until God gives me enough,
Power to stomp the enemy at a moments notice,
He flows through us and is in us,
Like hurricane gusts,
His grace overwhelms and overtakes us,
God is unstoppable and so are we,
If we believe that Greater is He that is in us,
Than he that is in the world,
All humanity and creation must bow down and worship,
The One who sent His Son,
We must press on and through like good soldiers,
With no notice, we receive papers for tours of duty,
That last until He calls us home,
We must know who we are and whose we are,
Identity is key in defeating the enemy,
It makes us free, not in bondage,
No more chains holding me down,
I can see clearly now, it is day,
I survived the night,
When no man can work, yet it hurts,
The process of purging and purifying,
You are dying daily,

Crying God save me from this death,
It is not His will for anyone to perish,
So cherish this moment,
That you are about to live,
And it's about to be on and I am not stoppin',
Until I get all my stuff.
They are my blessings.

Romans 10:9

If you confess with your mouth the Lord Jesus,
And believe in your heart that God raised Him from the grave,
You shall be saved,
You shall be saved,
If you are reading this message,
You can be protected from the grave,
Of never ending hell and spells,
And curses that follow you all the days of life,
You can have it more abundantly,
If you just believe and,
Repeat this message,
Lord Jesus, thank you for showing me how much I need you,
Thank you for dying on the cross for me,
I need and ask you,
To forgive all my failures and the sins of my past,
Make me clean and help me start fresh with you as my Dad,
I now receive you into my life as my Lord and Savior,
Help me to love and serve you,
It would be my pleasure,
With all my heart I thank you for receiving this, my prayer,
And saving me from the never ending hell and grave, Amen.
And if you are reading this message,
You have just been served Salvation papers,
And cannot say you have not heard,
About Jesus and what He did on Calvary,
Your assurance is guaranteed,
Only if you do not view these as vapors that disappear,

Not falling to the ground,

But snatched by the enemy,

Because you refuse to hear me or the knock at the door,

God is wanting to come in,

Only by invitation and,

If you seek His forgiveness,

Becoming a witness and receiving power,

He speaks louder and louder,

Through much difficulty and transgression,

Can you enter the Kingdom,

But it's no reason to reject the call to be saved,

Now you have a choice,

What and who will you believe.

Romans 10:9.

About the Author

MICHELLE ANDRE' CANNON is an author, poet, teacher, inspirational speaker and facilitator and entrepreneur. She has a Bachelor's degree in Business and a Master of Education degree from Concordia University Texas.

Her first book, My Damascus, has been featured in magazines and newspapers. Her speaking engagements have included Leadership Workshops, Conferences and Book Clubs.